# FRANCE

## ...in Pictures

Prepared by
**Geography Department**

**Lerner Publications Company**
Minneapolis

Independent Picture Service

**The owner of a small French hotel poses in the doorway with her cat.**

This book is an all-new edition in the Visual Geography Series. Previous editions were published by Sterling Publishing Company, New York City. The text, set in 10/12 Century Textbook, is fully revised and updated, and new photographs, maps, charts, and captions have been added.

Website address: www.lernerbooks.com

LIBRARY OF CONGRESS CATALOGING-IN-PUBLICATION DATA

France in pictures / prepared by Geography Department,
Lerner Publications Company.
    p.   cm. — (Visual geography series)
Rev. ed. of: France in pictures / by E. W. Egan.
Includes index.
Summary: Text and photographs present the topography, history, society, economy, and governmental structure of France.
ISBN 0–8225–1891–0 (lib. bdg.)
1. France—Juvenile literature. [1. France.] I. Egan, E. W., France in pictures. II. Lerner Publications Company, Geography Dept. III. Series: Visual geography series (Minneapolis, Minn.)
DC20.F744   1991
914.4'0022'2—dc20
                                            91–9149

International Standard Book Number: 0–8225–1891–0
Library of Congress Catalog Card Number: 91–9149

## VISUAL GEOGRAPHY SERIES®

**Publisher**
Harry Jonas Lerner
**Associate Publisher**
Nancy M. Campbell
**Senior Editor**
Mary M. Rodgers
**Editors**
Gretchen Bratvold
Dan Filbin
Tom Streissguth
**Photo Researcher**
Kerstin Coyle
**Editorial/Photo Assistants**
Marybeth Campbell
Colleen Sexton
**Consultants/Contributors**
Colette Saidane
Sandra K. Davis
**Designer**
Jim Simondet
**Cartographer**
Carol F. Barrett
**Indexer**
Sylvia Timian
**Production Manager**
Gary J. Hansen

Independent Picture Service

**A young girl carries home fresh baguettes — long loaves of bread that are part of almost every French meal.**

## Acknowledgments

Title page by Thomas Henion.

Elevation contours adapted from *The Times Atlas of the World,* seventh comprehensive edition (New York: Times Books, 1985).

2  3  4  5  6  7  8  9  10  –  JR  –  06  05  04  03  02  01  00  99  98

An imposing monument, the Arc de Triomphe commemorates the early nineteenth-century military victories of the French emperor Napoleon. The stone structure has stood at one end of the Champs-Elysées – a broad avenue in the French capital of Paris – since 1836.

# Contents

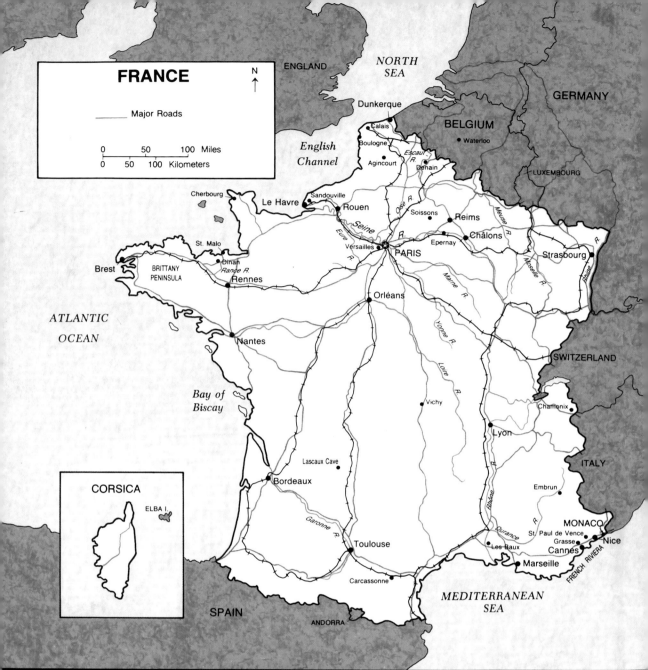

## FRANCE

N ↑

— Major Roads

0    50    100 Miles
0  50  100 Kilometers

ENGLAND

NORTH SEA

GERMANY

Dunkerque
Calais
Boulogne
BELGIUM
Waterloo
LUXEMBOURG

English Channel

Agincourt
Escaut R.
Denain

Cherbourg
Le Havre
Sandouville
Rouen
Oise R.
Soissons
Reims
Meuse R.
Châlons
Strasbourg
Rhine R.

St. Malo
Dinan
Rance R.
Seine R.
Eure R.
Versailles
PARIS
Epernay
Moselle R.

Brest
BRITTANY PENINSULA
Rennes
Marne R.

ATLANTIC OCEAN

Orléans
Yonne R.

Nantes

Loire R.

SWITZERLAND

Bay of Biscay

Vichy

Lyon

Chamonix

ITALY

Lascaux Cave

Bordeaux

Embrun

Garonne R.

Rhône R.

MONACO
St. Paul de Vence
Grasse
Nice
Cannes
FRENCH RIVIERA

Toulouse

Durance R.
Les Baux
Marseille

Carcassonne

MEDITERRANEAN SEA

SPAIN

ANDORRA

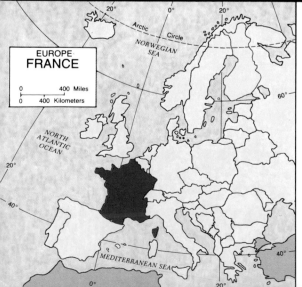

### CORSICA

ELBA I.

### EUROPE
### FRANCE

0    400 Miles
0  400 Kilometers

Arctic Circle
NORWEGIAN SEA

NORTH ATLANTIC OCEAN

MEDITERRANEAN SEA

### METRIC CONVERSION CHART
#### To Find Approximate Equivalents

| WHEN YOU KNOW: | MULTIPLY BY: | TO FIND: |
|---|---|---|
| **AREA** | | |
| acres | 0.41 | hectares |
| square miles | 2.59 | square kilometers |
| **CAPACITY** | | |
| gallons | 3.79 | liters |
| **LENGTH** | | |
| feet | 30.48 | centimeters |
| yards | 0.91 | meters |
| miles | 1.61 | kilometers |
| **MASS** (weight) | | |
| pounds | 0.45 | kilograms |
| tons | 0.91 | metric tons |
| **VOLUME** | | |
| cubic yards | 0.77 | cubic meters |
| **TEMPERATURE** | | |
| degrees Fahrenheit | 0.56 (after subtracting 32) | degrees Celsius |

A statue of the French king Louis XIV dominates the entrance of Versailles, a former royal palace near Paris. Expanded to magnificent proportions in the 1600s, Versailles is now a national museum and a popular tourist attraction. Its grounds cover 14,826 acres and contain parks, gardens, and elaborate fountains.

# Introduction

France, a large and populous nation in western Europe, has been an artistic center and a crossroads of trade for 2,000 years. The monarchs of France, who ruled the country until the French Revolution in the late 1700s, built a powerful colonial empire in many different regions of the world. At its height, the French Empire extended to North America, Africa, Asia, and the Pacific Ocean. After bringing down Europe's richest monarchy, the French Revolution led to political shifts in Europe.

France's standing among the other European nations also changed during the century that followed the revolution. Profits from trade became more important than territorial expansion, and competition for new markets often caused conflicts between France and its neighbors. As trade grew in France, so did industry. Factory workers in French cities became a powerful group, and these laborers influenced governments with their support or opposition.

In the 1800s and 1900s, a series of wars between France and Germany caused great damage and loss of life. In addition, by the mid-twentieth century, many French colonies had won their independence, ending France's overseas empire. Despite these changes and upheavals, France has maintained a strong economy, remaining a leader in industry, agriculture, and science.

The French are a traditional people who take great pride in their country's history and achievements. French is still an international language in business, politics, and science. The work of French writers, architects, and painters is admired throughout the world.

In the modern era, the French face the challenge of adapting to the European Union (EU). This organization hopes to unify the continent's economic markets by lifting trade barriers and creating a common currency. French leaders must find a balance between economic unity with the rest of Europe and their people's strong desire to preserve a separate French identity and culture.

The countryside of France has inspired artists for centuries. Here, a painter captures on canvas the cobblestone streets and old houses of St. Paul de Vence. The village lies near the resort town of Nice in southern France.

**Skiers skillfully maneuver down the twisting slopes near Chamonix in the French Alps, which form much of the country's southeastern border. During the summer months, mountain climbers scale the area's steep peaks, including Mont Blanc— the highest point in Europe.**

# 1) The Land

France covers an area of 211,208 square miles, which is about twice the size of the state of Colorado. Roughly six-sided in shape, France lies in western Europe. The country's longest distance from north to south is about 600 miles, and its greatest width from east to west is about 550 miles.

Most of France's borders run along natural barriers formed by mountains or water. The Pyrenees Mountains separate France from Spain and Andorra to the south. The Alps form France's frontier with Italy in the southeast, and the Jura range lines the frontier with Switzerland in the east. To the northeast lie Germany, Luxembourg, and Belgium.

Three seas also make natural boundaries for France. The Mediterranean Sea touches the country's southern coast. The English Channel—La Manche in French—separates Normandy in northwestern France from England. The Bay of Biscay, an arm of the Atlantic Ocean, stretches along the western coast. Sand dunes, marshes, rocky headlands, deep bays, and high limestone cliffs line many of the country's shores.

7

The blossoming trees of an orchard shade grazing cattle in Normandy, a region of gently rolling hills in northwestern France.

The island of Corsica, which lies in the Mediterranean Sea 100 miles off the southeastern coast, is also French. France continues to rule territories in the Caribbean Sea, in the Indian and Pacific oceans, and in South America.

## Topography

Although France contains several mountainous regions, most of the country is a series of gently rolling plains broken by river valleys, low ridges, and hills. The plains contain two large, roughly circular areas called basins. The Paris Basin stretches from Brittany in the northwest to the Vosges Mountains in the northeast. North of the Paris Basin are the flat low-

The Durance River begins in the French Alps and winds its way through the productive farming areas of southeastern France before emptying into the Rhône River.

Forests blanket the slopes of the nation's mountain ranges, which dominate eastern, central, and southern regions.

Photo © Russel Kriete/Root Resources

lands of Flanders, a region famous for its industrial and mining activities. The Aquitaine Basin in southwestern France extends southward from the central Loire River Valley to the Pyrenees Mountains.

Rugged mountains lie in the south, the southeast, and the east. The Pyrenees in southern France reach 10,000 feet and have prevented easy trade and transportation between France and Spain. Few passes have been cut through this range, which is home to one of Europe's last remaining populations of bears.

The French Alps begin near Nice, a city on the Mediterranean coast, and reach France's border with Switzerland. Located in the French Alps are many of Europe's highest peaks, including Mont Blanc. At 15,771 feet above sea level, Mont Blanc is the tallest point in France. Several mountain valleys in the high elevations near Mont Blanc contain glaciers (slow-moving masses of ice).

France also has several smaller mountain ranges. The Jura Mountains lie along the French-Swiss border. The Vosges

Boats carry people and goods along the Seine River, France's primary commercial waterway. It flows from the east central part of the country through Paris to the English Channel.

Mountains in the northeast have forested slopes and grassy, rounded summits. Another range occupies a high plateau in south central France known as the Massif Central. Extinct volcanoes rise above the surrounding plateau.

## Rivers

The winding rivers of northern and western France have long been important trade and transportation routes. An extensive network of canals joins rivers that flow west toward the Atlantic with waterways that empty into the Mediterranean. The canals also link France with inland water routes in other European countries.

The main river of this complex network is the 482-mile-long Seine, which begins in the Vosges Mountains. The Seine loops westward through the northern plains and empties into the English Channel near the port of Rouen. Barges carrying coal and other products share this busy river with private houseboats and water taxis. On several small islands in a wide spot in the river, the capital city of Paris was founded about 2,000 years ago. Many secondary rivers, or tributaries, flow into the Seine. The Marne and Oise rivers arrive from Flanders, and the Eure and Yonne rivers join the Seine from the southeast.

Through central France flows the wide, shallow Loire River. Rising in the southern Massif Central, the Loire travels 634 miles north and west before entering the Bay of Biscay near the city of Nantes. The nation's longest waterway, the Loire is famous for the châteaus (castles) and vineyards built along its banks. Large boats and barges cannot use the Loire, since many islands and shallow gravel banks exist throughout its course.

Another river known for the castles along its banks is the Rhine, which begins in western Switzerland and forms a portion of France's border with Germany. The Moselle River, a tributary of the Rhine, lies almost entirely within France. The Moselle, Meuse, and Escaut rivers link the nation with ports on the North Sea, into which the Rhine empties. Once a rapid and wild river, the Rhône River in southern France has been tamed by a series of dams that provide hydroelectric power and irrigation.

## Climate

The climate of any location in France depends on the place's elevation and its distance from the sea. Winds that blow inland from the Atlantic Ocean moderate temperatures on the western plains in both summer and winter. Coastal areas and northern peninsulas have a rainy climate year-round, with little change in temperature from season to season.

The annual rainfall in cities along the English Channel typically ranges from 39 to 47 inches. Farther inland—in Paris and the Paris Basin—summers are warmer and rainfall levels are lower. Paris has temperatures that average 37° F in January (the coldest month) and 65° F in July (the hottest month). Paris receives about 24 inches of rain throughout the year.

Seasonal differences in climate are greater in eastern France. Winters are cold in the Massif Central and in the mountainous border regions. In the Alpine town of Embrun, January temperatures average

During the winter months, villagers trudge through the snow that covers small resort towns in eastern France. Some Alpine areas receive more than 40 inches of annual precipitation.

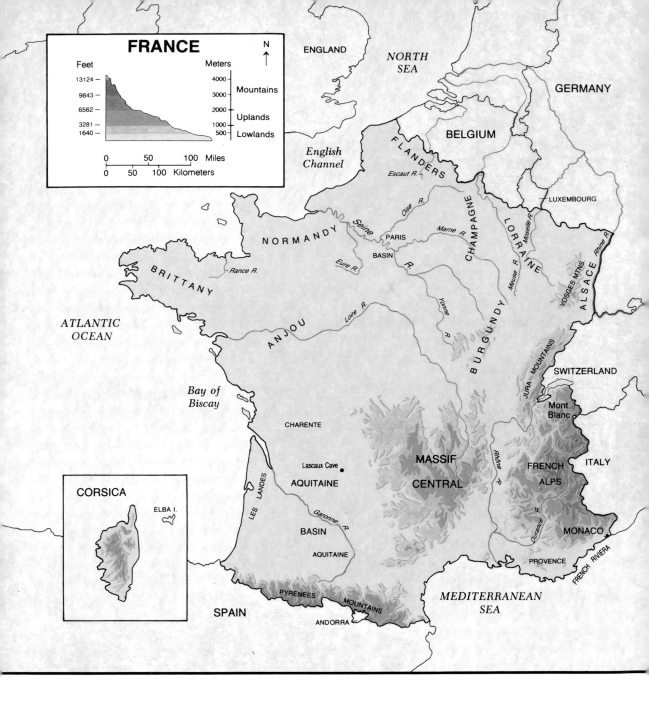

33° F, and in July they hover around 67° F. These highland areas receive an average of more than 40 inches of precipitation per year. At lower elevations in the east, rains are heaviest in summer. In winter, the mountains get much of their precipitation as snow.

A warmer and drier climate prevails along the Mediterranean coast, where winters are mild and summers are hot. During the winter, the Alps block cold weather from the region. At Marseille, a Mediterranean port, temperatures average 45° F in January and 68° F in July. Annual rainfall is 22 inches. Cool northerly winds called mistrals originate in central France and blow over the Mediterranean coast, sometimes causing crop damage.

## Flora and Fauna

France still has many of its original forests, which cover nearly one-fourth of the country's total land area. Walnut, oak, chestnut, beech, and ash trees grow in the carefully maintained forests of central and southern France. Poplars line many French highways, as well as the smaller roads that run from village to village. Pine forests thrive on the slopes of the Alps, of the Massif Central, and of the Jura and Vosges mountains.

At one time, laws set aside some forests for wealthy French people, who hunted the abundant game in the reserved woodlands. All French citizens can now enjoy these reserves, which have been made into game parks and hiking retreats. In southern France, olive trees and cypress pines flourish in the dry, warm climate. Lichens and mosses grow in the mountains at high elevations where trees cannot survive.

Photo © David Falconer

**Sports enthusiasts angle for the freshwater fish that populate the country's lakes, rivers, and canals.**

Photo by Drs. A. A. M. van der Heyden, Naarden, the Netherlands

**Thick forests have overtaken the ruins of an eleventh-century castle in southern France's Massif Central.**

Centuries of farming, hunting, and settlement have reduced France's population of large mammals. Deer and fox still inhabit the large forests of the plains. Wolves, bears, and a few wild boars survive in remote mountains, particularly in the Pyrenees. The chamois—a large, agile animal resembling an antelope—climbs the slopes of the Alps. Wild rabbits live along the sandy coastlines of Aquitaine and Normandy in northern France. Porcupines, weasels, red squirrels, pheasants, and wild turkeys flourish in less-populated regions of the country.

The last wild horses of Europe survive in La Camargue, a protected saltwater marsh located at the mouth of the Rhône River near Marseille. Cranes, herons, and other rare species of migratory birds also live in this nature reserve. Freshwater fish inhabit France's lakes and waterways. Fishing for pike, bass, and perch in lakes is a popular sport, and trout are caught in France's mountain streams.

13

The home of a variety of ethnic and religious groups, Marseille sits on France's southeastern coast. Tourists are attracted to the city's modern shops, beautiful churches, and Old Port where sidewalk cafes overlook a bay filled with pleasure boats. Marseille is also considered the home of bouillabaisse, a popular fish stew.

## Secondary Cities

The second largest city in France is Lyon (population 1.3 million), which has been an important urban center for more than 2,000 years. Located in the middle of the Rhône River Valley, Lyon is the hub of the French chemical industry. It is also an important city for the manufacture of textiles and automobiles. The first high-speed French train—named the Train à Grande Vitesse (TGV)—connected Lyon with Paris in 1983.

Marseille (population 1.1 million) is France's most important port and the country's third largest city. With its natural harbor, Marseille was the site of a Greek colony founded about 2,600 years ago. The city is home to a large population of immigrants, and commercial ships from around the world line the port's docks.

Old and new combine in Strasbourg, a river port in northeastern France. Factories in the city produce chemicals, metals, plastics, and textiles. Strasbourg is equally famous for its ancient buildings, including its fifteenth-century cathedral.

Colorful buildings, lively street life, and palm-lined avenues add to Marseille's attractions.

Toulouse (population 650,000) lies along the Garonne River in southwestern France. The home of the French aircraft industry, Toulouse has companies that are also an important part of Europe's aerospace program. Electronics, chemicals, and food processing are other industries in Toulouse. The buildings of the city's center were constructed in an unusually colored stone that has earned Toulouse the nickname "the pink city."

The Mediterranean port of Nice (population 517,000) is situated at the foot of the Alps near the Italian border. During the summer, the city attracts many French and foreign tourists with its fine hotels, wide beaches, and warm, dry climate. Factories in Nice produce perfumes, olive oil, soap, and cement. Nice is also the principal city of the French Riviera, a famous region of wealthy resort towns.

Other regional centers of France developed along major river valleys or on its seacoasts. For example, Bordeaux, a center of the French wine industry, lies on the Garonne River in Aquitaine. Strasbourg, a city on the Rhine, is the hub of France's river trade with the rest of Europe. Along the coast of the English Channel are Calais, Le Havre, and Cherbourg. These ports have commercial ties with England and serve fishing fleets, freighters, and passenger ships.

Cannes, located on the Mediterranean Sea, is known for its annual film festival, which features movies from all over the world. The city is one of several popular resorts on the French Riviera.

Using black, yellow, and red paints, prehistoric peoples in France decorated the Lascaux Cave with images of familiar animals, including horses and buffalo. The paintings, which are thousands of years old, were discovered east of the city of Bordeaux by a young French boy in 1940.

# 2) History and Government

Humans have inhabited the area of modern France for nearly 100,000 years. The earliest people in this part of Europe lived in caves and used stone weapons to hunt for food. These Stone-Age people left vivid cave paintings of the animals that they hunted.

Around 3000 B.C., the inhabitants of France began to develop larger communities near rivers and seas and to grow food crops. They buried their dead in underground rooms called dolmens and raised huge stone markers known as menhirs. Early farmers used the menhirs to keep track of the seasons. The arrangement of the stones in relation to the stars guided the farmers to plant and harvest their crops at the right time.

About 800 B.C., hardy warriors called Celts invaded France from the east. The Celts soon gained control of most of the European continent. Mounted on horseback, they defeated their enemies with iron weapons and superior numbers. In time, however, the Celtic population grew too large to survive on the conquered lands. While moving south to settle more territory, the Celts made contact with people from Greece and Rome—two powerful civilizations of southern Europe.

## Rome and Gaul

In the second century B.C., Rome was an expanding republic with a large, well-equipped army. The Romans took control of Marseille, then a Greek trading port, in 121 B.C. Roman settlers soon established other colonies in the region, which the Romans called Gaul. The fertile plains of Gaul offered Rome space for its rapidly growing population.

In 58 B.C., the Roman general Julius Caesar invaded Gaul with a large army. Caesar's purpose was to defeat the Celts and to claim Gaul for Rome. Under the Celtic leader Vercingetorix, the Celts resisted Caesar but could not unify their forces to drive away his army. The war continued until 52 B.C., when the Romans defeated the Celts at the Battle of Alesia in the region of Burgundy. The victors took Vercingetorix prisoner, and Celtic resistance to Rome ended.

The Romans soon colonized nearly all of Gaul. Roman engineers built roads and cities in the province, and many Roman citizens established large farming estates. The Celts adapted well, becoming successful traders and farmers and learning the Latin language of the Romans. In time, the people of Gaul also accepted Christianity, which became the official Roman religion in the fourth century A.D. For several centuries, Gaul enjoyed peace and prosperity.

By the middle of the fifth century A.D., however, the Roman Empire was in decline. A variety of non-Christian warriors—mainly Visigoths, Franks, and Burgundians—began invading Gaul from eastern Europe. Their raids weakened Rome's hold on the province.

A more serious danger threatened Gaul about A.D. 450, when Huns from Asia attacked. Under their leader, Attila, the Huns burned and looted farms, villages, and cities as they pushed westward. To stop the Huns, the Frankish, Visigothic, and Burgundian armies in Gaul joined with the Roman legions. Together they defeated Attila at the Battle of Châlons in 450. After the battle, however, Roman control of Gaul weakened further.

After losing the Battle of Alesia in 52 B.C., the Celtic chieftain Vercingetorix *(left)* surrendered to the Roman general Julius Caesar. Caesar took his Celtic captive to Rome, where Vercingetorix was displayed as a symbol of Caesar's triumph. The Romans executed the chieftain in 46 B.C. to stop a renewal of Celtic resistance to Roman rule.

**19**

In the fifth century A.D., the Franks invaded what is now France under their leader Clovis (on horseback). He converted to the Christian faith in 496 and made the people in his empire accept the religion as well.

Photo by Bettmann Archive

## Merovingians and Carolingians

In the decades after Attila's downfall, the Franks dominated the area of Gaul between the Rhine and Loire rivers. In 486 Clovis, the leader of the Franks, defeated a Roman army at Soissons and conquered northern Gaul, which he called Francia. A clever and ruthless leader, Clovis united many different Frankish groups and founded the Merovingian dynasty (family of rulers). When Clovis abandoned the Frankish religion and became a Christian in 496, the Frankish Empire became Christian as well. The center of Christianity was in Rome, and the Roman Catholic Church guided the faithful.

After the death of Clovis, his empire was divided among his four sons. This division of property was customary but led to countless quarrels as Clovis's heirs fought to extend their territories. Although Francia grew to include areas in the south and east, the divided Merovingian dynasty became increasingly weak.

Control of the realm's everyday affairs passed to the mayors of the palace, who were the principal advisers of Merovingian kings. Pépin of Herstal, the strongest of these mayors, was a skilled military commander who brought the different states of Francia under his authority. By the time he died in 714, Pépin had established a strong kingdom, which his son Charles inherited.

Charles was nicknamed Martel, meaning "hammer," because of his success in battle. He gained the support of the Roman Catholic Church after preventing an attack on Rome by the Lombards of northern Italy. After this action, the church allied itself more closely with the Frankish rulers.

### CHARLEMAGNE

The son of Charles Martel established the Carolingians as the new dynasty in Francia. Charles's grandson, also named Charles, conquered the Saxons, Bavarians, and Avars, all of whom lived east of the Rhine. In southern France, the younger Charles stopped North African invaders called Moors, who had conquered Spain and Portugal.

Charles was an energetic ruler as well as a successful military campaigner. He divided his many conquests—which included much of Germany, northern Italy, and nearly all of what is now France—into smaller regions. To administer each region, Charles appointed a loyal governor. In 800 he traveled to Rome with his army to settle a dispute between Roman officials and the Catholic pope (leader). Charles peacefully resolved the disagreement in the pope's favor. In gratitude, the pope crowned Charles emperor of western Europe. From then on, Charles was known as Charlemagne (Charles the Great).

Charlemagne held together his large empire with his personal skill and authority. In 814 Charlemagne died, and his realm was divided among his heirs. Lands west of the Rhine became the property of Charlemagne's grandson Charles the Bald. This realm, called the West Frankish Kingdom, is the ancestor of modern France.

The power of the Carolingian monarchs weakened through the late ninth and early tenth centuries. The Carolingians were also unable to stop the Vikings—sea raiders from northern Europe. Rich landowners built castles for protection and employed private armies. In time, these nobles became the independent rulers of the areas that surrounded their castles. In return for protection from raiders, farmers worked the nobles' land. They also promised their loyalty and gave the nobles a percentage of their crops. The property and wealth of these landowners increased their influence over the monarchs of France, whom the nobles elected.

## The Capetian Dynasty

The Carolingian dynasty ended in 987, when the nobles chose Hugh Capet as king. Capet was a powerful duke whose

**By the late 700s, another Frankish commander named Charles had taken over present-day France, Germany, and northern Italy. He had strong ties to the Roman Catholic Church, and its leader Pope Leo III crowned Charles emperor of western Europe on December 25, 800. Thereafter, he was called Charlemagne (Charles the Great).**

**21**

DIN ANTES ET CVNAN C LAVES POR REXT

Panels from the Bayeux Tapestry, an eleventh-century embroidered wall hanging, show scenes from French history and everyday life. Here, French nobles fight for control of the city of Dinan. After Conan, the duke of Brittany *(right, on horseback)* was defeated, he yielded the keys to the city gates to his opponent William, duke of Normandy.

lands lay between the cities of Paris and Orléans to the south. Although the nobles believed they had selected a man they could easily control, Capet arranged for his own son to inherit the French throne. This move began the Capetian dynasty in 996. Under the Capetians, the nobles continued to rule their own lands and were called upon to serve the monarch only in wartime.

By the twelfth century, the Capetians had begun to extend their holdings. Louis VII, who reigned from 1137 to 1180, greatly expanded royal territory when he married an heiress named Eleanor of Aquitaine in 1137. But the couple only had daughters, and Louis divorced Eleanor in 1152 so that he could remarry and possibly have a son to inherit the throne.

Louis VII, who belonged to the Capetian family of rulers, owned a large area of France in the 1100s. French nobles, as well as the king of England, also held power over parts of France at this time. The lack of unified government resulted in prolonged conflicts over territory in later centuries.

The vast lands of Aquitaine, however, still belonged to Eleanor, who then married Henry, a nobleman from Normandy. When Henry became king of England in 1154, Eleanor's property became English land. Ownership of Aquitaine caused disputes between England and France for many centuries.

Philip II became king of France in 1180 and further expanded royal power through marriage and military conquests. His new possessions included Normandy and Anjou in northern France. In the southern region of Provence, religious rebels angered the Catholic pope, who summoned a crusade (religious war) against them. Philip II and his successor, Louis VIII, sided with the pope and brought Provence under the control of the French king.

Louis IX, successor to Louis VIII, was a deeply religious man as well as a practical ruler. Louis appointed local judges to settle disputes and to hear complaints. He earned the loyalty of the French people with his fair system of government. As a sign of his devotion to the church, Louis ordered new cathedrals and religious monuments to be built in many French cities. He also led religious crusades to the Middle East and to Africa, where he died in 1270. After his death, Louis was named a saint by the Roman Catholic Church.

Philip IV, who reigned from 1285 to 1314, tried to bring the church under royal control. He also increased his authority over local officials, judges, and tax collectors. Philip called together a parliamentary group known as the Estates-General in 1302. Made up of landowning nobles who supported Philip's reforms, the Estates-General laid the foundation for a later French legislature.

## The Hundred Years' War

In 1328 Philip's successor, Charles IV, died without an heir. Charles's cousin, Philip of Valois, inherited the throne as Philip VI. The new king became the first member of the Valois dynasty. Philip had

The fleur-de-lis, meaning "flower of the lily," became a symbol of French kings in the twelfth century. According to legend, an angel gave the flower to Clovis when he accepted Christianity in 496. The name Clovis is an early version of Louis, and the French monarchs bearing this name gradually brought the fleur-de-lis into use on their royal banners and shields.

Artwork by Laura Westlund

to compete with another claimant to the French throne—Edward III, king of England. A direct descendant of the Capetian Philip IV, Edward felt he was entitled to reign over France as well as England. To back up his claim, Edward invaded Normandy in 1337, sparking a war that was to last more than 100 years.

The Hundred Years' War began with English victories at sea and at the French port of Calais. France was further weakened when a deadly disease, called the Black Death, broke out in Marseille in 1348. Rats on ships arriving in the port had carried the disease to Europe. Within a few years, the plague had killed nearly one-third of the inhabitants of France.

The last half of the fourteenth century was a time of unrest, disease, and warfare. Prices rose, and roaming bands of soldiers robbed towns and estates throughout the kingdom. The French king John II was captured by the English, and the French paid a huge ransom for his release. Another king, Charles VI, reigned for 42 years while suffering from long periods of mental illness. After Henry V of England defeated the French armies at Agincourt in 1415, most of France fell under English control. Charles VII, who succeeded Charles VI in 1422, became a king without a realm, wandering from city to city while English armies controlled the countryside.

France's situation was bleak in the 1420s when Joan of Arc, a peasant girl from the province of Lorraine, arrived at Charles's court. Claiming to be guided by angels, Joan changed the course of the Hundred Years' War. Her strong devotion to the Catholic church and to the king inspired French soldiers to take the offensive against the English. She personally led the army to victory at Orléans in 1429.

This battle was the first of many English defeats that gradually pushed the invading armies to the coast. Joan, however, was captured by the English and executed, becoming an important symbol of French resistance. Eventually, Charles VII drove the English out of most of France, and the Hundred Years' War ended in 1453.

## Recovery and Rebirth

During the rest of the fifteenth century, the population and economy of France recovered from the many years of plague, starvation, and war. Charles's successor, Louis XI, expanded his authority over French nobles. The king claimed the right to impose and to raise taxes. He also increased the territory of his kingdom and created a permanent army.

By the early 1500s, peace and the economic policies of the French kings had fostered a growing middle class of merchants and bankers. An artistic movement called the Renaissance (meaning "rebirth") began in Italy and spread to France with the encouragement of King Francis I.

Courtesy of Philadelphia Museum of Art, SmithKline Beckman Corporation Fund

**A woodcut portrays a patient suffering from the plague. This disease, sometimes called the Black Death because black spots of blood formed under the victim's skin, claimed the lives of one-third of France's population in the 1300s.**

The historian Jean Froissart *(seated left)* wrote a four-volume chronicle of the Hundred Years' War (1337–1453) in the 1300s. This illustration from Froissart's work shows the French queen Isabella of Bavaria, wife of Charles VI, traveling through Paris, whose ancient buildings stand in the background.

During the Hundred Years' War, French and English armies clashed on French soil. France lost ground until the 1420s, when a young French girl, Joan of Arc, convinced the king that her religious visions could lead to victory. She urged French troops under her command to keep fighting, and they won several important battles. Captured in 1430, Joan went on trial *(above)* in front of English nobles and Roman Catholic officials, who accused her of being a witch. Although Joan defiantly affirmed that her visions came from God, the court found her guilty of witchcraft and burned her at the stake in 1431.

He supported the work of skilled French artists, writers, and architects.

Also in the early 1500s, a movement for religious reform—known as the Protestant Reformation—was introduced to France through the teachings of John Calvin, a Swiss preacher. The French Protestants, called Huguenots, gained many followers.

The French monarchs and the Catholic church saw the Huguenots as a serious threat to royal authority. The kings' attempts to destroy the French Protestants deepened the divisions within French society. A religious civil war began in the late sixteenth century. Many people on both sides of the conflict were killed. In 1572 Roman Catholics attacked a crowd of Protestants in Paris and killed nearly 2,000 people.

Three of Francis I's grandsons ruled in succession under the guidance of their mother, Catherine de Médicis. In 1589 the last grandson was assassinated, leaving no

Louis XIV ruled France from 1643 to 1715. His ambition—to make his kingdom the most powerful realm in Europe—led him to participate in a series of European wars. During his long reign, Louis built the magnificent palace at Versailles to display his wealth and to keep a close eye on the nobles who came to his court. Throughout this opulent era, however, the standard of living for ordinary citizens declined, and this change caused deep discontent among the population.

Henry of Navarre (1553–1610) spent his early life engaged in religious and political wars. Raised as a Protestant, he formally embraced the Roman Catholic religion in 1593, a few years after he became king of Catholic-dominated France. Once peace was established, Henry began a long program of economic and financial recovery that was cut short by his assassination in 1610.

direct heir. The Huguenot leader Henry of Navarre, a descendant of the saintly king Louis IX, took the throne. To calm Catholics who did not want a Protestant king, Henry converted to Catholicism in 1593. The first ruler of the Bourbon dynasty, Henry granted freedom of religious worship in 1598.

France became strong again under Henry, who reformed the economy and constructed new roads and canals. He reduced taxes on the common people and weakened the nobility's hold on the land.

## Expansion in the 1600s

Henry was assassinated in 1610, and nine-year-old Louis XII became king. He governed with the help of a powerful adviser, Cardinal Richelieu, who was determined to concentrate power in the hands of the king. To achieve this, Richelieu ordered the destruction or seizure of many castles and estates. The king named royal representatives to oversee the courts and to collect taxes. France's income increased as French ships and merchants established trade with ports in North America and Africa. These early links eventually led to the founding of overseas colonies.

Richelieu also allied France with the Netherlands and Sweden against the growing power of the Habsburg monarchs in Austria. This alliance won the Thirty Years' War, which lasted from 1618 to 1648. After the war, France gained new territory along the Rhine and strengthened its existing borders.

But the French kings soon became unpopular. High taxes and poor harvests were bringing misery to the countryside. By 1643, when Louis XIV inherited the crown, a widespread rebellion had erupted. This revolt, called the Fronde, was stopped in Paris by the royal army. The popular rebellion convinced the king that the growing middle class and the nobility were too powerful. As a result, Louis XIV took personal control of the kingdom.

Louis wanted to make France the world's richest and most powerful nation. Protective trade policies strengthened the French economy, and new roads and canals linked the provinces to one another. In 1700 French armies attacked Spain and the Netherlands to expand French territory and to place Louis's grandson on the Spanish throne.

Although most of Louis XIV's military campaigns were successful, they drained the kingdom's resources. Louis deprived Huguenots of their rights and finally canceled their guarantee of religious freedom. As a result, several hundred thousand Huguenots—who made up an important class of merchants and traders—emigrated to Europe and North America. This loss further weakened the French economy.

The left and right panels of a tapestry show the surrender in 1704 of the French to the English after the Battle of Blenheim (now in Germany). The battle was part of England's effort to stop Louis XIV's territorial expansion in Europe. As a result of his defeat, Louis had to give up some French-held lands in North America.

Living conditions worsened in France in the late 1700s under Louis XVI. On July 14, 1789, Parisians stormed the Bastille, a fourteenth-century stronghold used as a prison. Their success in destroying the structure—a hated symbol of royal power—heralded the beginning of the French Revolution. This rebellion overthrew the monarchy and set up a republic (a government that has no king).

Independent Picture Service

## The French Revolution

After reigning for 73 years, Louis died in 1715, leaving the throne to his five-year-old great-grandson, Louis XV. The country was then at the height of its strength and dominated the affairs of Europe. A huge fleet of trade ships helped France control one of the world's largest colonial empires. French became the international language of business, science, and diplomacy. French writers were famous throughout Europe for their new ideas of equality and civil rights.

At the same time, however, heavy taxes and poor harvests brought hardship to French laborers. Corrupt royal officials used their jobs to make themselves rich. Louis XV was unwilling to address these problems or to adapt the French economy to changing conditions. The growing middle class, along with members of the nobility, demanded better government and a greater voice in running the country.

Louis XVI, who inherited the throne in 1774, attempted some reforms, but his administrators opposed them. The king's control of the government weakened as he failed to make much-needed political and financial changes. Trade competition from other European powers also weakened the French Empire. Violent demonstrations

occurred in the countryside, and the public called for a representative assembly. These events made Louis summon the Estates-General in 1788.

This assembly, inactive since 1615, was made up of members from the clergy (the First Estate), the nobility (the Second Estate), and the middle class (the Third Estate). Soon after the assembly's first session in 1789, the representatives of the Third Estate formed the National Assembly and wrote a new constitution. When Louis attempted to disband this new assembly, Parisians stormed and captured a prison called the Bastille on July 14, 1789, touching off the French Revolution. The revolution continued in Paris and spread to the provinces. The king's troops, who were outnumbered by the demonstrators, were put on the defensive.

Meanwhile, the National Assembly decreed sweeping changes in French government and society. The legislature stripped the nobility of their vast lands and fired corrupt provincial judges and tax collectors. The assembly also took away lands belonging to the Catholic church. This action, as well as other changes in France, angered the pope.

France became divided between forces loyal to the king and those defending the

The early governments of the French republic were unstable. Here, an angry mob confronts the leaders of the revolution. One member of the crowd carries a sign in French that says, "Homeland, Equality, Freedom." These social aims—to establish a free nation with democratic representation—also inspired revolutions in other European countries.

authority of the National Assembly. The nation also faced invasion from Britain and from the Habsburg kingdom, which opposed the revolution. Habsburg armies invaded France in the spring of 1792. After the Habsburg forces defeated the French, another internal revolt brought down Louis and the Bourbon monarchy. He and his Austrian queen, Marie-Antoinette, were executed in 1793. The National Assembly then established the First Republic (a government without a king).

Rebel leaders sent Louis XVI, his wife Marie-Antionette, and their children to a French prison in 1792. The king was tried for treason, was convicted, and was executed in 1793. During the Reign of Terror that followed, thousands of people—including Louis's queen—were beheaded at the guillotine in Paris.

## The First Republic and Napoleon

The formation of a republic and the election of a new assembly—the National Convention—did not stop the widespread unrest and foreign invasions. To establish order and to eliminate those who still supported the monarchy, some members of the new assembly formed the Committee

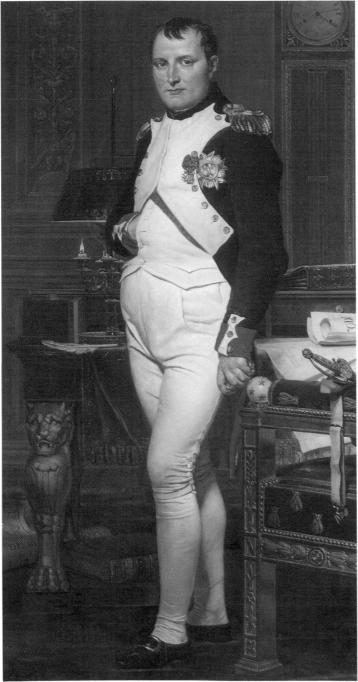

The French artist Jacques-Louis David painted the French emperor Napoleon Bonaparte in 1812, when Napoleon was at the height of his power. Born on the island of Corsica, Napoleon trained as a soldier in the French army and rapidly came up through the ranks in the 1780s. By the time of the revolution, he had impressed French leaders with his military genius. In 1799, after Napoleon had taken over the army and government, he proceeded to subdue other European countries in a string of decisive battles. Yet the young emperor did not neglect problems within France. He ordered a new law code to be written, redrew local boundaries, and improved the economy. By 1812 Napoleon controlled territory that stretched eastward from Spain to Poland and southward from Norway to Italy.

Photo © Kenneth Rapalee/Root Resources

A display at Waterloo in Belgium shows the final battle between French troops under Napoleon *(on the white horse)* and the Europeans allied against him. The allies won the fight on June 18, 1815, ending the French emperor's career and military ambitions.

of Public Safety. It executed thousands of commoners, nobles, and clergy during a period called the Reign of Terror, which lasted until 1794. Meanwhile, the new government's troops turned back the foreign armies.

In 1795 the National Convention drew up a new constitution. It established a five-member directory and two legislative houses to run the country. Although these changes brought France some political stability, the nation experienced four more years of unrest and violence. French people who wanted the monarchy to return opposed the new regime. Dissatisfied with the Directory, they supported an energetic young general, Napoleon Bonaparte, in his bid to overthrow the republic in 1799.

### NAPOLEONIC RULE

A brilliant military and political planner, Napoleon took control of the army and the government. Under his direction, lawyers put together the Napoleonic Code as the country's new set of laws. It established freedom of speech, freedom of religion, and freedom to choose a profession. The new government completely overhauled the economy and replaced the royal treasury with the state-owned Bank of France.

To reestablish French military power in Europe, Napoleon successfully invaded Italy and the Habsburg lands of central Europe. The rulers of these states quickly asked for peace terms. Napoleon also settled trade and military conflicts with Britain and reached an accord with the Catholic church. Through these agreements, he gained time to plan for his actual goal—the creation of a French Empire that would dominate the continent.

After proclaiming himself emperor of France in 1804, Napoleon again invaded central Europe. His enemies quickly drew together in a strong coalition to oppose him. Britain controlled the seas, blocking French ports and France's valuable trade with its colonies. Napoleon's unsuccessful attack on Russia destroyed his largest and best army. The alliance's forces drove Napoleon from Germany in 1813, and the emperor surrendered in 1814. The victorious nations placed the younger brother of Louis XVI, Louis XVIII, on the throne, restoring the Bourbon monarchy.

The nations allied against Napoleon had exiled him to the Italian island of Elba. In March 1815, however, he returned to France at the head of a powerful French army. The allies assembled near the Belgian town of Waterloo and defeated Napoleon on June 18, 1815. The emperor

Louis Philippe, who reigned as king of France from 1830 to 1848, acquired his throne partly through Talleyrand's diplomatic skills. Known as the "citizen king" because he accepted many democratic principles, Louis Philippe ruled within limits imposed by a written constitution.

Once a political ally of Napoleon, Charles-Maurice de Talleyrand-Périgord deserted the emperor in 1807. After Napoleon's defeat at Waterloo, Talleyrand attended the postwar Congress of Vienna and ably represented the interests of a defeated France. Late in his life, Talleyrand guided French revolutionaries toward the establishment of a constitutional monarchy.

surrendered to the British, who sent him to the remote island of St. Helena, where he died in 1821. For the second time, the allied nations decided that their best chance for peace was to restore Louis XVIII to the throne of France. They also stationed military troops in France to keep the population under control.

## The Nineteenth Century

Although at peace, France was now divided between Royalists, who backed the king, and Republicans, who supported the Chamber of Deputies (a representative assembly). The nation slowly recovered from Napoleon's wars. Charles X, who became king in 1824, established a stronger central government. He curbed many personal liberties, including the right to vote, dissolved the Chamber of Deputies, and ordered new elections. The three days of riots in Paris that followed these actions forced the king to give up his throne in

1830. The chamber chose Louis Philippe of the Bourbon family to be the new king.

During the reign of Louis Philippe, France rapidly became more industrialized. New factories and manufacturing methods transformed the economy. Workers moved from villages and farms to large cities. The government built railroads and schools. The monarchy, however, refused to give workers the right to vote.

In the towns and cities, the people's desire for their own representatives increased as the nation entered an economic depression in 1846. In 1848 a street demonstration in Paris turned into a widespread, violent revolt. This time, the rebels overthrew both the constitution and the king, and Republican leaders established the Second Republic.

After the 1848 revolution, demands for further social reforms continued, and outbreaks of urban violence became common. Republicans retained control of the government and adopted a new constitution. It established voting rights for all male citizens as well as an elected president and an elected one-house assembly. Napoleon Bonaparte's nephew, Louis Napoleon, won the first presidential election but feared the assembly would limit his power. He overthrew the constitution and proclaimed himself Emperor Napoleon III.

### THE THIRD REPUBLIC

Napoleon III fostered further economic development. He encouraged trade with other nations and authorized public-works projects in the countryside and in the larger

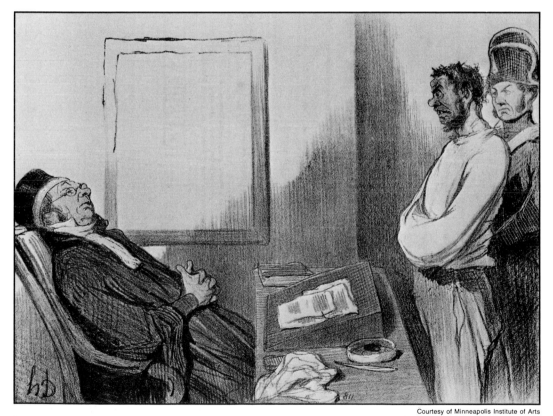

Courtesy of Minneapolis Institute of Arts

In his many cartoon-like images, the French artist Honoré Daumier criticized French society and its prejudices. Here, a judge (left) considers the plea of a man arrested for stealing food. The caption in French (not shown) translates, "You were hungry . . . you were hungry . . . That's no reason . . . I myself am hungry almost every day and I don't steal for that!"

Soldiers in World War I (1914–1918) huddled behind the remains of a bombed-out forest to avoid German artillery fire. French, British, U.S., and other allied nations fought in northern France during this global conflict. The fighting was so prolonged that local economies were shattered, and the woods, farmland, and property of war-torn regions were completely destroyed.

Courtesy of National Archives

cities. These changes were part of the widespread industrialization of Europe.

Meanwhile, Prussia (part of modern-day Germany) was building an army and was attempting to unite the German states into a powerful empire. To curb this threat, France declared war against Prussia in 1870. The French armies were quickly defeated, and Napoleon III surrendered himself and his forces to the Prussians. Prussia forced France to give up Alsace and Lorraine, two important provinces of northeastern France.

French officials formed the Third Republic after the defeat, creating a representative body called the National Assembly. Although disputes between Republicans and Royalists continued throughout the 1880s, further social improvements were made. Industry expanded in the late nineteenth century. Workers formed labor unions, and the government made schooling free and compulsory for all children of primary school age.

During this time, France gained two important allies by signing pacts with Russia in 1894 and with Britain in 1907. The alliance of these three European powers—called the Triple Entente—was intended to balance the rising military strength of Germany. Under Prime Minister Otto von Bismarck, Germany soon created a three-member alliance of its own with Italy and Austria.

## The World Wars

A confrontation between the two alliances broke out in 1914. France, Britain, and Russia were soon at war with Germany and Austria. (Italy sided with the Entente powers.) German troops crossed Belgium into northern France, where the opposing armies fought to a standstill.

Throughout four years of fighting, neither side gained a decisive victory. Not until 1918 were the combined forces of Britain, the United States, and France able to drive back the German army. On November 11, 1918, Germany surrendered. Northern France had suffered widespread damage, and nearly 1.5 million French people had been killed.

### BETWEEN THE WARS

Under the terms of the Treaty of Versailles, signed in 1919, Germany gave Alsace and Lorraine back to France. The treaty also demanded that Germany pay France huge sums of money for damages caused by the war.

Determined to avoid another European war, French officials signed several peace treaties, including the Kellogg-Briand Pact of 1928. The government rebuilt the French army and strengthened fortifications—called the Maginot Line—along the German border to stop any future attacks from the east.

France enjoyed stability and prosperity until 1932, when a worldwide economic depression hit the French economy. Rising unemployment and factory closings led to strikes and violence by members of the country's labor unions. Many dissatisfied French people joined the Popular Front—an alliance of politicians from the Radical, Socialist, and Communist parties. The Popular Front won a majority of seats in the National Assembly in the elections of 1936.

Under the leadership of Léon Blum, this government granted many of the workers' demands, including a shorter, 40-hour workweek. Blum also faced an increasing military threat from Germany, which had been under the leadership of Adolf Hitler since 1933. Hitler was rebuilding Germany's industries to manufacture new tanks, airplanes, and warships.

France remained closely allied with Britain in the decades after World War I. But their combined power did not stop Hitler from adding Austria to Germany in 1938 or from invading Czechoslovakia in 1939. The French and British governments tried to prevent war by allowing Hitler to keep the lands he invaded, but their strategy

**World War II in Europe and North Africa**

Legend:
- Allied Nations
- Axis Nations
- Axis Occupied Areas
- Vichy France
- Neutral Nations
- → Major Allied Advances

Artwork by Laura Westlund

In World War II (1939–1945), France again was at war against Germany. The Germans invaded France in May 1940, and the French government surrendered in June. The victors occupied the northern two-thirds of France, while in the south a French regime friendly to Germany was installed at Vichy. This government not only ruled unoccupied France but also administered French colonies in North Africa and the Middle East.

failed. In the summer of 1939, German tanks, airplanes, and infantry quickly conquered Poland, an ally of Britain and France. By September 1939, the Second World War had started in Europe.

### WORLD WAR II

In May 1940, German tanks invaded northern France, and within weeks, Paris had fallen. The French government asked for peace, signing a truce with Germany on June 17. When the French surrendered, Germany took direct control of two-thirds of the country. Other provinces, in the south and southeast, remained under a French administration headquartered at Vichy. The Vichy government, which was led by Marshal Henri Pétain, offered no resistance to the occupying German forces.

Meanwhile, a French general named Charles de Gaulle had escaped to Britain and had formed the Free French movement. He urged all French soldiers to join him to fight against the German occupation. Fighters in France struggled in secret against the Germans, who built a series of defenses along the country's northwestern coast. The defenses were designed to stop any sea invasion by the Allies. This group included Britain, the United States, and Canada.

In 1944 Canadian, U.S., and British forces gathered in Britain and prepared to attack the European continent along the French coast. Arriving on June 6, 1944, the allied armies fanned out from the beaches of Normandy, liberating Paris on August 26. De Gaulle returned to the capital and organized a government. After the surrender of Germany in May 1945, de Gaulle established the Fourth Republic and became its first president.

## Postwar Development

Once in power, de Gaulle demanded more authority. The members of the National Assembly disagreed with him, and the crisis forced de Gaulle to resign a year later. After the temporary presidency of Georges Bidault, Vincent Auriol was elected president in 1947. René Coty succeeded Auriol in 1953.

In the 1940s and 1950s, France turned its energies toward rebuilding its economy and improving its social-security system. Although France made some progress at home, postwar relations with its colonies worsened. Indochina, a large French territory in Southeast Asia, revolted in 1946. By 1954 defeats had forced the French to grant self-rule to Laos, Cambodia, and Vietnam—three new countries carved out of Indochina.

At the same time, the North African colony of Algeria rebelled. Conflict between military and political leaders over the Algerian war eventually caused the Fourth Republic to collapse in 1958. De Gaulle came out of retirement to run a temporary government. A new constitution in-

U.S. soldiers wade through hip-high water to reach the beaches of Normandy in northern France. This allied land invasion in 1944 led to the liberation of the entire country from German control.

In the 1950s, France fought an unsuccessful war against local forces in the Southeast Asian colony of Indochina. Here, French soldiers fire a cannon on rebel troops. After the war, the French colony was divided into the nations of Vietnam, Cambodia, and Laos.

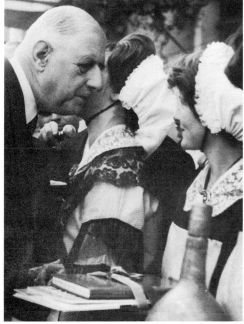

During a national campaign, French president Charles de Gaulle received a kiss from a supporter dressed in the traditional costume of Provence. De Gaulle's popularity rose and fell during the 1960s, until he resigned from office in 1969.

creased the authority of the president and established the Fifth Republic. Voters elected de Gaulle, head of the Gaullist party, to a seven-year term as president.

Civil war raged in Algeria until a cease-fire was finally established in 1962. De Gaulle urged the National Assembly to recognize Algerian independence. Although the French army resisted this move, the public supported it. After Algeria became an independent nation, about one million French colonists and Algerians settled in France.

De Gaulle, who was reelected to another term as president in 1965, turned his attention to rising prices and unemployment. These problems affected young university students, who felt that the country's economy could not provide them with suitable jobs and incomes. In 1968 student demonstrations in Paris led to widespread strikes and violence throughout the country.

De Gaulle called for new elections, in which the Gaullists won a majority of seats in the National Assembly. But in 1969 voters strongly rejected two major changes to the constitution that de Gaulle had proposed. Because of this loss of support, he resigned the presidency and retired permanently from politics.

De Gaulle's prime minister, Georges Pompidou, succeeded him as president after winning national elections in June 1969. Although Pompidou promised to continue some of de Gaulle's policies, the new president faced serious economic problems. The cost of oil rose sharply when oil-producing Arab countries increased their prices. France, which imported most of its petroleum, had to adjust to a critical shortage of fuel. Unemployment was still rising, and the prices of goods threatened to spiral out of control. Pompidou died in 1974, leaving these problems unsolved.

Photo by Drs. A. A. M. van der Heyden, Naarden, the Netherlands

**Surrounded by uniformed soldiers, François Mitterand, who won his first term as France's president in 1981, participates in a Bastille Day parade that honors the eighteenth-century French Revolution.**

## Recent Events

The Independent Republican party and its leader, Valéry Giscard d'Estaing, won the elections called to replace Pompidou. Promising to resolve disputes among the French leaders, Giscard invited other political parties into his government. In 1976 he named Raymond Barre, who had few political ties, to be prime minister. The person in this post has broad powers to direct day-to-day governmental affairs. A skillful economic planner, Barre reduced the government's control of the national economy. For example, he withdrew state support for private companies that were struggling to succeed.

Barre's policies were only partially successful, and Giscard lost the presidential election of 1981. French voters chose a leader from the Socialist party, François Mitterand, as president. Mitterand soon gave the direction of the French economy back to the government. Banks and large industries were nationalized (placed under

state control). Higher taxes paid for increased welfare benefits.

Because of attempts by the Socialist government to change the French economic system, support for Mitterand's party dropped in the late 1980s. To pass legislation, the Socialists often had to get votes from members of smaller parties.

Unemployment, slow economic growth, and inflation continued to plague France in the mid-1990s. The economic problems led to the defeat of the Socialist party in the 1995 presidential election. Jacques Chirac, the conservative mayor of Paris, succeeded Mitterand as president. Although Chirac promised economic reform, many of his efforts were blocked by trade unions and by opponents in the legislature, who strongly defended traditional social spending.

Chirac's problems mounted in 1997 when he called a surprise legislative election that brought defeat for his own party. Socialist party leader Lionel Jospin be-

38

came the new prime minister. The major challenge now facing the French coalition government is the planned common currency, called the "euro," for members of the EU. In order to qualify for the currency, France and other EU members must trim their budgets—a task that means cutting back the social benefits favored by French voters.

## Government

Citizens over the age of 18 elect the president of France every seven years. According to the constitution of the Fifth Republic (adopted in 1958), the president has the power to call new elections and to propose treaties and constitutional amendments. The chief executive may also take control of the government during national emergencies.

The president selects the country's prime minister, who is usually a political ally of the president. The prime minister oversees the government's various functions and directs the president's Council of Ministers, which is made up of the heads of government ministries.

The country's Federal legislature is made up of the National Assembly and the Senate. The 577 delegates in the National Assembly are elected to five-year terms by the voters in their districts. Elected by regional and city representatives, the Senate is a 321-member advisory body. The Senate may delay legislation, but final authority on the passage of new laws rests with the National Assembly.

France's judicial system is based on the Napoleonic Code, which was written under the direction of Napoleon in the early 1800s. Local courts exist in each region. Judges hear appeals from these tribunals in courts of appeal. The Court of Assizes hears all major criminal cases. France's highest court, the Court of Cassation, can review cases and return them to any of the lower courts.

France has 96 local administrative units, called departments, which include the 2 departments of the island of Corsica. Commissioners of each department are appointed by the national government. The residents of each department elect a local council to oversee the department's everyday affairs. The smallest units of government in France are the 36,673 communes, which are cities, towns, and rural communities. Each commune has a council and a mayor.

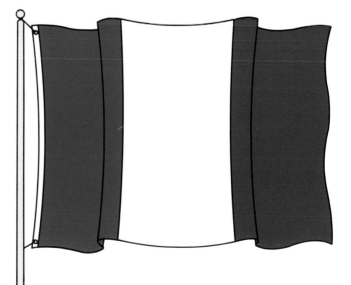

The three-part French flag, called the tricolor, dates from 1789, when the blue and red insignia of the revolution was combined with white—the still-legal symbol of royalty. Although the proportions of the three stripes have varied in the last 200 years, the tricolor has inspired the design of many flags around the world. The tricolor also flies over French possessions in South America, Asia, and Africa.

Artwork by Laura Westlund

Young French citizens take advantage of the excellent alpine skiing conditions. Many people conquer the slopes at an early age and enjoy the sport throughout their lives.

Courtesy of French Government Tourist Office

# 3) The People

About 74 percent of the 58.6 million inhabitants of France live in cities and towns of at least 2,000 people. Urban areas dominate the country's northern half, which has a higher population density than southern France has. In the north, French workers hold jobs in the industry and service sectors. South of the Loire River, many people are employed in agriculture and live on farms and in small villages. The overall population density of France is about 277 people per square mile.

## Ethnic Identity

Most French people have a mixed European heritage. The Celts—the first group to dominate the area that became France

—intermarried with Roman and Germanic settlers. Various regions of France have absorbed other ethnic groups as well. Viking invaders from Norway and Denmark left descendants in Normandy. Northeastern France, including Alsace, is home to many people of German background. The Bretons of the Brittany Peninsula have maintained their distinctive Celtic language, local cuisine, and traditional clothing. The Basques of southwestern France also have their own language, and many of them have joined with Spanish Basques in demanding a separate nation.

During the twentieth century, a shortage of workers attracted thousands of immigrants to France from Africa and southern Europe. After Algeria won its independence in 1964, nearly one million French colonists and Algerians moved to France. Many other North Africans have also arrived, either as war refugees or as laborers seeking work on farms and in factories. Competition for jobs and high unemployment have caused friction between these immigrants and the French in Marseille and in other large urban areas.

## Health and Welfare

France has a comprehensive social-security system that provides health insurance and other benefits for nearly all citizens. The plan pays for medicine, medical treatment, and hospitalization. Depending on a patient's income, the government covers up to 100 percent of these costs. Families receive allowances based on the number of children within each household. The government also funds other forms of social welfare, including support for the unemployed, for the disabled, and for retired people. The government has set a minimum wage and requires employers to grant at least four weeks of vacation per year to workers.

Because of improvements in national health-care services, the French are living longer than ever before. Life expectancy

French youths gather near a colorful sculpture at Les Halles in Paris. The late twentieth century brought increased ethnic diversity to France's urban areas as thousands of immigrants flocked to the country in search of a better life. In recent years, however, violence against minority groups has caused deep divisions within French society.

This steelworker in Denain benefits from generous government employment policies, including a minimum wage, four weeks of guaranteed vacation, and unemployment insurance.

at birth is now 78 years. France has had a rather high birthrate throughout the twentieth century. The current rate—12.2 births per 1,000 people—is still among the highest in western Europe. The number of babies who die within the first year is 5 per 1,000—an average figure among western European countries.

The recent spread of acquired immune deficiency syndrome (AIDS) has caused concern among doctors and government officials in France. French physicians were among the first to isolate and identify the AIDS virus, and the Pasteur Institute in Paris remains a leading center for the treatment of the disease.

## Education and Language

France has a comprehensive public education system. French nursery schools are free and available to children between the ages of two and six. Compulsory education begins at age six in the elementary schools. When they reach eleven, French students enter a *collège* for four years of schooling in a nationwide curriculum.

The *lycée* is a three-year high school that prepares students either for the university system or for vocational and technical training. Students who intend to enter the university system must pass a difficult examination called the *baccalauréat,* which nearly one-third of all candidates fail. About 20 percent of French students attend private schools, which are under the direction of the Roman Catholic Church.

About 1.5 million students attend French universities. A famous institution in this system is the University of Paris, which was founded in the 1100s. Other universities offer instruction in various professional fields. For example, the Collège de France focuses on literature. The Ecole Normale Supérieure prepares students for jobs as professors or government officials.

Photo © Andrew E. Beswick

**A group of elderly French people savor a bright, spring day in Nice. Retirees enjoy the advantages of the government's social-security system and health-care coverage.**

These children attend school in Strasbourg. One afternoon per week, students leave their classes for organized sports, musical instruction, and special-interest activities. To make up for missed study time, the children attend school on Saturday mornings.

At every level of schooling, classes are conducted in French. The language developed from the Latin tongue that was once spoken throughout the Roman Empire. The Celts adopted Latin and introduced their own words, as well as their own style of pronunciation. Later, the Franks and related Germanic peoples also influenced the early forms of French.

Around A.D. 1000, two main dialects of Old French arose—*langue d'oeil* in the north and *langue d'oc* in the south. These dialects were named for words meaning "yes"—*oeil* in the north and *oc* in the south. Contact with various civilizations brought words from Greek, Latin, Spanish, and Italian into Old French. Gradually, the language spoken around the city of Paris became the accepted form among writers, diplomats, businesspeople, and members of the royal court.

Although langue d'oc became the less commonly used dialect of French, it survives today as Provençal, the second language of many people in southern France. Other languages in France include Breton, a Celtic language spoken in Brittany, and Alsatian, which is a German dialect used in Alsace. The Basque language has survived in southwestern France.

## Religion

Throughout most of French history, the Roman Catholic Church has been closely tied to French education and family life. Although there has been no official state religion in France since 1905, 75 percent of the French are baptized as Roman Catholics. The nation observes many Christian holidays, including Christmas, Easter, and All Saints' Day (November 1). About one million Protestants live in France, and most of them belong to the Reformed (Calvinist) Church. Lutherans and Baptists belong to other important Protestant sects,

**43**

and the Russian and Greek Orthodox churches also have French members.

Many of the North Africans who immigrated after World War II follow the Islamic faith, which has about two million followers within France. Roughly 500,000 Jews live in the nation, and large Jewish communities exist in Paris and Marseille. Many of France's Asian immigrants follow the Buddhist faith.

## Literature

Literature has long had an important place in French culture. France's earliest poets were wandering minstrels, who composed and performed songs in castles and towns. Narrative poems of noble deeds, such as *The Song of Roland*, entertained French monarchs and their courts. In the fifteenth century, literary and scholarly works of the French Renaissance took ideas from ancient Greek and Roman writers. Fran-

Independent Picture Service

Built in the twelfth century, the Roman Catholic Cathedral of Notre Dame (Our Lady) in Paris is dedicated to the Virgin Mary. Notre Dame was the site of many important events in French history. For example, in the cathedral Henry VI of England was crowned king of France during the Hundred Years' War, and Napoleon I became emperor of France in 1804.

çois Rabelais's five-part story *Gargantua and Pantagruel* made fun of religious and social institutions. Michel de Montaigne described his life and thoughts in a new form called the essay.

The seventeenth century was a golden age of poetry and drama in France. The dramatists Pierre Corneille and Jean Racine wrote tragedies based on ancient Greek and Roman myths. The playwright Molière was supported by King Louis XIV and his court, even though Molière's comedies criticized and made fun of French aristocrats. René Descartes and Blaise Pascal were two important philosophers who wrote during this era.

During the eighteenth century, French writers believed that the use of reason could solve social and philosophical problems. In novels and essays, Voltaire and Jean-Jacques Rousseau wrote in favor of

Independent Picture Service

Considered one of the great writers of comedy, Molière experimented with many forms, including farce, satire, and comedy-ballet. One of his favorite themes was the contrast between how people view themselves and how others see them. An accomplished actor and director, Molière also held a law degree and brought his experience of everyday life into his hilarious plays.

civil rights for all citizens. The *Encyclopédie* of Denis Diderot classified and explained knowledge and discoveries in many different scientific fields.

After the French Revolution, some French writers turned away from political ideas and emphasized feeling over the use of reason in their works. Victor Hugo excelled at many literary forms. His two great works of historical fiction—*The Hunchback of Notre Dame* and *Les Misérables*—are set in Paris.

Other French writers of the 1800s wrote more realistic novels based on the social problems of their times. Honoré de Balzac and Gustave Flaubert favored realistic descriptions of French society. Emile Zola's series of novels portrays the members of a large family. Many talented French poets —among them Charles Baudelaire, Paul Verlaine, Stéphane Mallarmé and Arthur Rimbaud—also gained prominence in the late 1800s.

Leading writers of the early twentieth century, including André Gide and Paul Claudel, broke free of the styles and forms used by previous French writers. Marcel Proust's *Remembrance of Things Past* is a seven-part autobiographical work containing deep insights into psychology and society. Exploration of the mind also fascinated other writers in the 1920s and 1930s, including Louis Aragon and André Breton.

**Set in Paris, Victor Hugo's masterpiece *The Hunchback of Notre Dame* recounts the tale of Quasimodo, the cathedral's deaf and deformed bell ringer. He rescues Esmeralda, a beautiful gypsy dancer who has been unjustly accused of witchcraft. To protect Esmeralda, Quasimodo hides her in the belfry, but she is eventually executed. Quasimodo avenges Esmeralda's death by throwing her accuser from the cathedral's high bell tower.**

Flowers from appreciative readers adorn the grave of Sidonie-Gabrielle Colette, an early twentieth-century French writer of novels and short stories. Colette used her writings to explore human nature, especially the emotional impact of love and jealousy on female characters.

After World War II, writers found new material in the problems and questions of individual freedom, existence, and morality. Jean-Paul Sartre and Simone de Beauvoir were the leading thinkers of this new philosophy, which became known as existentialism. Sidonie-Gabrielle Colette wrote a large number of novels during the first half of the twentieth century. Albert Camus, a French writer from Algeria, questioned modern government, religion, and society in his novels, plays, and essays. Other French novelists—including Alain Robbe-Grillet, Marguerite Duras, and Claude Simon—prefer to experiment with the form and style of the traditional novel.

## The Arts

Painting in France flourished during the Renaissance, when wealthy French aristocrats invited Italian artists to beautify castles and palaces. Italian painting also influenced the seventeenth-century French artists Georges de la Tour and Nicolas Poussin. In the eighteenth century, painters used elaborate detail to depict domestic scenes and mythological subjects for their aristocratic patrons. In the early nineteenth century, the artists Eugène Delacroix and Jacques-Louis David often used huge canvases to portray historic events.

Paris became an international center of painting in the late 1800s, when French artists brought impressionism to the French capital. This method of painting allowed artists to experiment with light and color on their canvases. Among the most famous French impressionists were Edouard Manet, Claude Monet, Pierre-Auguste Renoir, and Paul Cézanne. Several twentieth-century artistic movements, such as cubism, dadaism, and surrealism, began in Paris. These new forms left the rules of conventional painting behind, focusing instead on abstract shapes, playful imagery, and unusual techniques.

The French musical tradition began with the songs of the troubadours (singer-poets) and the *chansons de geste*, long narratives created between the eleventh and the thirteenth centuries. Music for religious ceremonies dominated the work of French composers during the Renaissance. Later,

Together with Claude Monet, Pierre-Auguste Renoir developed the technique of impressionism. These artists blurred the outline and form of their subjects to allow the viewer's eye to define the image. Renoir is famous for his richly colored works, such as *Oarsmen at Châtou (left),* that depict French middle-class life.

Courtesy of Minneapolis Public Library and Information Center

during the reign of Louis XIV, Jean-Baptiste Lully combined dance, drama, and music into large-scale productions. These spectacles developed into a French style of opera, which became an important musical form. In the 1700s, Jean-Philippe Rameau added extravagant staging to his operas. He also developed new theories about how to write music. These ideas are still followed by many composers.

The opera and the symphony influenced French musicians during the nineteenth century. Hector Berlioz, the creator of *Symphonie Fantastique,* was one of Europe's leading composers. Other important writers of symphonies were Camille Saint-Saëns and Gabriel Fauré. Georges Bizet composed the music for *Carmen,* which has remained one of the world's most popular operas.

Many French musicians were also influenced by impressionism. Claude Debussy's piano works caused a sensation with their unusual scales and harmonies. Maurice

Paul Cézanne created works that hover between the realistic and the abstract. His style influenced many other leading French painters, including Georges Braque and Henri Matisse.

Courtesy of Minneapolis Public Library and Information Center

**47**

The French composer Claude Debussy (1862–1918) revolu-tionized orchestral music with his nontraditional harmonies and forms. The work of writers and artists inspired Debussy, who based his famous piece *Prelude to the After-noon of a Faun* on a French poem by his contemporary, Stéphane Mallarmé.

Known for his straw hat and charm, Maurice Chevalier began his career in 1901 and gained fame in the mid-1900s as an actor and singing comedian. He starred in 12 U.S. films, including *Gigi,* which was taken from a story by Colette.

The Georges Pompidou Center, named after the president of France from 1969 to 1974, shrugs off the traditional image of a museum. The architects, Richard Rogers and Renzo Piano, created a futuristic design that places the stairs, escalators, heating and cooling shafts, and water and gas pipes on the outside of the building. Their plan allows the inside space on each floor to be used completely.

Ravel, who often drew upon musical forms from earlier centuries, paved the way for new composing techniques that arose in the 1920s and 1930s.

France has a rich tradition of folk and popular music. The singers Edith Piaf, Maurice Chevalier, and Yves Montand achieved great popularity after World War II. Serge Gainsbourg, who started as a jazz pianist in Parisian nightclubs, was one of France's biggest musical stars until his death in 1995. Other contemporary French musicians, among them Pierre Boulez, are creating new electronic music.

French architects pioneered many building techniques in the nineteenth and twentieth centuries. For example, cast iron was first used in the construction of the Eiffel Tower, which was built as a temporary structure for the Paris World's Fair of 1889. The tower still stands near the banks of the Seine in Paris. Le Corbusier was a twentieth-century pioneer in the design of both private and public buildings.

Controversial architectural styles have sometimes appeared in the French capital. The designers of the Georges Pompidou Center, an art museum built in the 1970s, caused debate by using a unique combination of glass and steel to expose normally hidden parts of the building's interior.

**Designed by Alexandre-Gustave Eiffel, the Eiffel Tower was built over several years in the late 1880s. The 982-foot, 7,000-ton structure is held together by 2.5 million rivets and requires 50 tons of paint when it is repainted every seven years.**

## Food

French cooking has been world renowned for centuries. Yet an ordinary meal prepared in a French home is likely to be simple. The main meal of the day has several courses. Soup or an appetizer precedes meat or fish, which may come with potatoes, rice, or fresh vegetables. A garden salad follows the main course. Several varieties of cheese, each from a different region of the country, are served before a dessert—sometimes pastries, crêpes (a kind of pancake), or fruit. A crusty loaf of French bread, called a baguette, accompanies the meal.

Appetizers are an important part of the French menu. Pâté de foie gras is a delicate spread made from goose liver. Escargot are snails from Burgundy cooked in butter, parsley, and garlic. Truffles—black mushrooms dug up by specially trained pigs—are a rare and expensive delicacy.

The abundance and variety of meat and fresh produce in France is the basis for many regional specialties. These dishes include cassoulet—a stew of white beans, pork, chicken, and sausage cooked in tomato sauce—from the region of Toulouse. Bouillabaisse, a thick fish soup from Marseille, and Alsatian choucroute—

Courtesy of California Strawberry Advisory Board

**Desserts, such as these strawberry-stuffed crêpes, provide a sweet finish to a satisfying French dinner. Similar to very light pancakes, crêpes are prepared in a special pan that cooks them evenly without burning.**

**Creamy soups, like this potato-and-leek soup, are often the first course of the main meal. Soups also make a filling dish by themselves when served with a baguette.**

which is made with various meats and sauerkraut—make filling meals by themselves. Favorite seafoods include oysters, mussels, shrimp, crab, lobster, trout, bass, perch, and pike.

French wines accompany all courses of a traditional main meal. Many of the red wines from Bordeaux and Burgundy are world famous. White wines from the Loire Valley and rosé wines from Anjou often accompany fish courses. A small region east of Paris produces excellent champagne for festive occasions and for family celebrations.

**The French, who favor fresh ingredients in their recipes, make daily trips to the *marché* (street market) and the *pâtisserie* (pastry shop).**

Photo by Velo News/Cor Vos

Cyclists from all over the world compete in France's most grueling sporting event, the 2,500-mile Tour de France. Here, Greg Lemond – the winner of the 1990 race – leads the way through the rugged French Alps.

Independent Picture Service

Opponents stretch for the soccer ball during a tough match. Fans of the most popular team sport in France cheer their regional teams to local or national victories.

## Sports and Recreation

The varied terrain of France offers a wide range of sports and leisure activities. Downhill and cross-country skiing are popular in the mountains. In the summer, many French people hike or climb in the Alps, the Pyrenees, or the Massif Central. Swimmers and sunbathers crowd the long seacoasts along the Mediterranean and the Atlantic Ocean during the summer. The game of *pétanque* is played year-round in parks and town squares throughout the country. In pétanque, two teams compete in throwing small metal balls at a distant target. Tennis, fishing, handball, and ice-skating are other popular activities.

France's low-lying countryside is ideal for bicyclists. Although automobiles have taken over the country's roads, many people still use bicycles to travel short distances. Bicycle racing is one of the country's favorite sports. The Tour de France,

Independent Picture Service

Daring downhill skiers brave the steep runs that line France's snow-packed mountains.

52

the world's most famous bicycle race, is a grueling, three-week test of cyclists' strength and endurance.

Soccer—called *football* in France—remains the country's most popular team sport. Rugby, which is similar to U.S. football, is popular in the south, and France's national rugby team often competes in international championships. The French also enjoy basketball and volleyball. There is a growing interest in U.S. team sports, especially football and baseball, and amateur teams play these new sports in the larger cities.

Residents of a small village in southern France enjoy a round of *pétanque,* a game that resembles bowling. Pétanque, also called *boules,* is usually played on a rough surface. The object of the game is for the members of a team to toss their balls closer to a tiny target ball, called a *cochonnet,* than the opposition does.

**Wearing special gear that provides protection from hot sparks and flames, a French foundry worker supervises the production of molded metal products, called castings. France is one of the world's leading manufacturers of metal goods.**

# 4) The Economy

Once a largely agricultural nation, France rapidly industrialized in the early twentieth century. The world wars, however, stopped the nation's economic expansion. After World War II ended in 1945, government programs rebuilt important industries, constructed housing, and improved services. The state took control of banks and the transportation system.

France experienced rapid growth until the late 1970s, when greater overseas competition and higher energy costs slowed the economy. To survive, many small, family-owned companies merged into larger firms. Heavy industries, such as steel and automaking, cut costs by streamlining production. Both of these trends caused unemployment to rise.

France has a broad economy, and French people enjoy a high standard of living. France has also been a force in the European Union's efforts toward a common market. French planners expect the European common currency, the euro, to lower the costs of selling French goods and services abroad.

At the same time, the euro brings daunting problems. Government budget deficits must be less than three percent of GDP (gross domestic product—a measure of a country's wealth) to qualify for the euro. That will mean cuts in social spending as well as reductions in government spending and support for French companies. France must create jobs through economic growth or risk social unrest.

## Manufacturing and Trade

With careful planning and extensive foreign aid, France rebuilt many damaged and destroyed factories after World War II. Governmental control of major industries helped the nation to supply essential products during the postwar era. Manufacturing now employs about 20 percent of the country's workers. France's major industries make vehicles, steel, and chemicals.

The French automobile industry is now the fourth largest in the world after those of the United States, Japan, and Germany. Auto plants in Paris, Rennes, Strasbourg, and Lyon produce more than three million cars each year for export and for domestic sale. Aircraft and aerospace equipment also have become leading industries, especially in Toulouse. The transportation sector ranks highest in total value of finished products.

The country's iron and steel factories are concentrated in eastern and northern France. Much of the iron ore necessary for the production of steel is mined in Lorraine. New steelworks on the Mediterranean coast and in Dunkerque contribute to the country's annual output of 17 million tons of steel.

Textiles, a traditional French industry, still provide a livelihood for nearly 250,000 workers. Shops in various regional centers

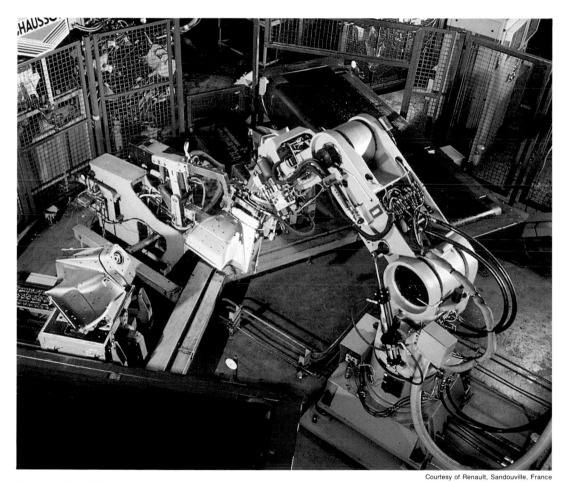

Courtesy of Renault, Sandouville, France

**At an auto plant in Sandouville, in northern France, computer-controlled robots efficiently perform a variety of tasks, such as welding, drilling, and painting car parts.**

**55**

In southeastern France, workers in Grasse, the country's perfume capital, sift through mounds of flower petals that have been collected from vast gardens in the south. The petals are steamed or boiled to obtain the oils used in scenting perfume, cologne, soap, and paper.

Independent Picture Service

weave wool, cotton, silk, and synthetic fibers into cloth. Factories in the Paris region supply finished clothing. Fine perfumes, made from flowers grown in southern France, also come from Paris.

Services, such as banking and insurance, have become an important part of the French economy. Nearly one-fourth of all French workers provide services, which make up nearly two-thirds of the country's gross national product (the value of all goods and services produced by a country in a year).

France imports much of the fuel it needs for domestic and industrial use and exports automobiles, chemicals, textiles, aircraft, and agricultural products. Besides the United States, France's most important trading partners are EU members, including Germany, Italy, the Netherlands, Britain, and Belgium. Almost half of all French exports go to other EU countries.

## Agriculture

Agriculture in France employs 6.8 percent of the country's work force. Farming benefits from a mild climate, fertile soil, and the economic support of the French government. Small farms once dominated French agriculture, but many family farms have been combined into larger estates. The average French farm is still family owned and usually covers about 70 acres.

**Cattle graze on some of the grasslands that cover about one-fourth of France's land area. The country is one of Europe's largest agricultural producers, and two-thirds of the nation's farm income comes from meat and dairy goods.**

Roughly 35 percent of the land in France is under cultivation.

Nearly two-thirds of all agricultural income results from meat and dairy production. France has more than 21 million cattle, 17 million pigs, and 11 million sheep. The country is a leading producer of milk and cheese, which come from farms in the mountainous areas of the east and south and from Normandy. The grasslands of northern and western France make good pasture for horses, which are bred for work, recreation, and competitive racing.

Farmers plant wheat, barley, and corn in northern and central France. Sugar beets rank second to wheat in volume. Other vegetable crops include potatoes, carrots, tomatoes, and cauliflower. Fruit orchards, olives, and sunflowers thrive in the dry climate of southern France.

Grapes also flourish in the south and are used to make the fine French wines that are famous throughout the world. Wine grapes grown in Bordeaux, the Loire Valley, Burgundy, and the Rhone Valley thrive in the dry, well-drained soils of these regions. The government strictly controls wine-production methods.

**The temperate climate in some areas of France is ideal for growing grapes used to make wine. Workers harvest the grapes by hand, and machines crush the fruit to release the juice, which then ferments in large wooden vats or metal tanks before bottling.**

## Mining and Energy

French supplies of coal, once a major fuel for homes and industries, are declining. The coal-mining regions of northern France suffered when other fuels, such as oil, began to provide heat and electricity. Although France has petroleum refineries, it must import most of its crude oil from the Middle East. Oil fields in Les Landes and natural gas from the Pyrenees meet some of the country's energy needs.

France has been a leading producer of bauxite since the discovery of this mineral near the French town of Les Baux in the nineteenth century. Bauxite is an important component of aluminum production. Alsace and Lorraine provide potash and phosphates, which are refined into agricultural fertilizers. Salt, taken from mines and evaporated from seawater in factories along the coast, is used in food processing. French mines also produce zinc, lead, iron ore, and gold.

The French government supports an extensive nuclear power program, which now provides about 80 percent of the nation's electricity. Some 56 reactors are in operation, and others are planned. Hydroelectric dams and power plants on the Rhone and other rivers of southern France also produce electricity. The world's first tidal plant, built in 1966 on the Rance River in Brittany, uses the high tides near the port of St. Malo to generate power.

Hydroelectric dams harness some of the energy of France's many waterways. As rushing water enters the power station, it turns the blades of a large wheel, called a turbine. A long shaft attached to the turbine drives a generator that produces electricity for nearby homes and businesses.

Photo by The Hutchison Library

## Fishing

France's principal fishing ports, including Boulogne and Brest, lie along the coasts of Normandy and Brittany. More than 10,000 fishing boats ply coastal waters, as well as more distant areas in the North Atlantic Ocean. The catches include cod, herring, tuna, whiting, sardines, and a variety of shellfish.

France is a leading European exporter of lobsters and oysters. Oyster farmers in the regions of Charente and Les Landes use salty lagoons to raise oysters for sale at home and abroad. Freshwater fish, such as carp and trout, are also commercially raised on nearly 300,000 acres of specially constructed farms. The fishing industry of France employs more than 75,000 workers and brings in an annual catch of 867,000 tons.

## Transportation

France has one of Europe's most extensive and modern road networks. Expressways connect the principal cities, while national and departmental roads serve smaller towns and villages. Workers have blasted tunnels through mountains to build highways in the Alps near the Italian border. An underwater tunnel linking France and Britain was begun in 1988. Completed in 1994, this Eurotunnel under the English Channel offers an important connection between the two countries for both cars and trains.

France's state-owned railroad system serves most cities and towns. In mountainous regions, where rail construction is difficult, buses connect train stations to remote villages. The high-speed TGV first ran between Paris and Lyon in 1983. The TGV now carries passengers between many cities in France at speeds that exceed 100 miles per hour.

The two airports in the Paris region, Orly and Charles de Gaulle, are among the world's busiest landing fields. Air France is the country's international airline. For domestic flights, travelers use Air Inter.

**59**

Traveling at a top speed of 235 miles per hour and at an average speed of 170 miles per hour, the TGV is Europe's fastest train. Since 1983 the TGV has zipped between France's major cities, offering passengers an efficient mode of transportation.

The French can journey to almost any destination on the country's extensive network of roads, but in the center of Paris traffic jams hamper urban travel.

The French Concorde is a supersonic jet that can take passengers from Paris to New York in only three hours.

## Tourism

Approximately 35 million visitors from all over the world vacation each year in France, and tourism adds about $21 billion annually to the country's economy. The principal attractions are the city of Paris, the Mediterranean and Atlantic coasts, and the river valleys, especially the Loire Valley. Nature reserves in the Pyrenees and in the Massif Central attract hikers, climbers, and campers. Huge theme parks near Paris—Disneyland Paris and Parc Astérix —attract millions of international visitors.

The French government actively promotes tourism by planning and building resorts in popular tourist areas. The French Riviera, on the Mediterranean coast, has long been a favorite spot for visitors. Many new hotel complexes are also under construction on the Atlantic coast of Aquitaine in southwestern France. In Paris, tourists seeking fine music and art can visit the new Bastille Opera or the Musée d'Orsay, a former train station that now houses nineteenth-century sculpture and painting.

The ancient town of Carcassonne lies between Toulouse and the Mediterranean Sea. Although Carcassonne has two sets of defensive walls, it has been attacked and leveled several times in its long history.

Independent Picture Service

Courtesy of Tom Streissguth

I. M. Pei's outdoor pyramid (left) provides light for underground public-service areas in the Louvre Museum, one of Paris's biggest tourist attractions. The Louvre's outstanding collection of artwork includes Leonardo da Vinci's painting *Mona Lisa* and the Greek sculpture *Venus de Mllo.*

The firm of Moët & Chandon has made fine champagnes for many decades. The company's cellars at Epernay in northeastern France draw visitors every year, and a nearby museum recounts the history of champagne production.

Independent Picture Service

Photo by Thomas Henion

To honor Saint Michael, Norman-French Catholics built the abbey of Mont St. Michel in Normandy between the eleventh and sixteenth centuries. The religious site rests 250 feet above sea level on a giant mound of granite. At high tide, about one mile of water separates Mont St. Michel from the French mainland. A causeway links the ancient town to nearby land. Over the years, river-borne silt has accumulated near the site, so that high tides do not always reach the town's walls.

Photo by Drs. A. A. M. van der Heyden, Naarden, the Netherlands

Notre Dame was one of the first cathedrals designed with flying buttresses. These arched supports strengthen outer walls that contain heavy, stained-glass windows.

Photo by Christine Pemberton/The Hutchison Library

The French island of Corsica, located in the Mediterranean Sea between southeastern France and northwestern Italy, displays a wide variety of landscapes, including mountains, deserts, and beaches.

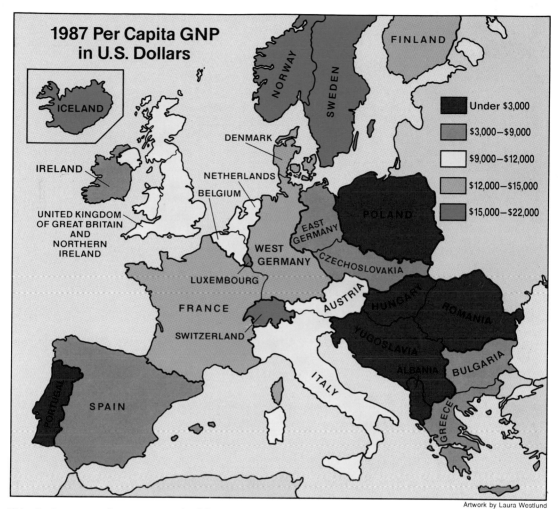

**1987 Per Capita GNP in U.S. Dollars**

Legend:
- Under $3,000
- $3,000–$9,000
- $9,000–$12,000
- $12,000–$15,000
- $15,000–$22,000

Artwork by Laura Westlund

This chart compares the average productivity per person—calculated by gross national product (GNP) per capita—for 26 European countries. The GNP is the value of all goods and services produced by a country in a year. To arrive at the GNP per capita, each nation's total GNP is divided by its population. The resulting dollar amounts are one measure of the standard of living in each country. France's GNP in 1995 was $24,990—double the figure from a decade ago. Membership in the European Union has helped to boost France's wealth by allowing the country to participate in many regional economic opportunities.

## The Future

Rising prices and high unemployment continue to affect the French economy. France's economic future depends largely on the country's ability to adapt to opportunities that develop in Europe in the next century. With a skilled labor force and a sound banking system, France is in a strong position to benefit from European unification.

Politically, however, the Fifth Republic is at a stalemate. Socialists hold a large number of seats in the National Assembly, while a Conservative president directs the various governmental ministries. Although French leaders often dispute internal goals for the nation, they agree on the need to seek a strong political and economic voice for France in future European affairs.

# Index